W.E.B. DuBOIS

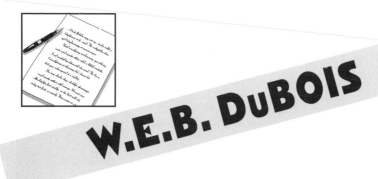

W.E.B. DuBois

Scholar and Civil Rights Activist
by Melissa McDaniel

A Book Report Biography
FRANKLIN WATTS
A Division of Grolier Publishing
New York / London / Hong Kong / Sydney
Danbury, Connecticut

Cover illustration by Bob Conge, interpreted from a photograph
by © New York Public Library Picture Collection

Photographs ©: Archive Photos: 49; Brown Brothers: 70; Corbis-Bettmann:
62 (Underwood & Underwood), 58, 65, 67, 86 (UPI), 25, 34, 38, 44, 80; New
York Public Library Picture Collection: 15, 17, 53, 55; Schomburg Center for
Research in Black Culture: 23 (Illustration by John Henry Adams), 12, 21;
Special Collections and Archives, W.E.B DuBois Library, University of Mas-
sachusetts, Amherst: 2, 9, 13, 27, 29, 40, 84; The Library Company of
Philadelphia: 36.

Visit Franklin Watts on the Internet at:
http://publishing.grolier.com

Library of Congress Cataloging-in-Publication Data

McDaniel, Melissa.
    W. E. B. DuBois : scholar and civil rights activist / by Melissa
McDaniel.
        p. cm.—(Book report biography)
    Includes bibliographical references and index.
    Summary: Examines the life of the African American scholar and
leader who helped establish the NAACP and devoted his life to gaining
equality for his people.
    ISBN 0-531-11433-3 (lib. bdg.)
    1. DuBois, W. E. B. (William Edward Burghardt), 1868–1963—Juve-
nile literature. 2. Afro-Americans—Biography—Juvenile literature. 3.
National Association for the Advancement of Colored People—Biography—
Juvenile literature. [1. DuBois, W. E. B. (William Edward Burghardt),
1868–1963. 2. Civil rights workers. 3. Afro-Americans—Biography.] I. Title.
II. Series.
E185.97D73M43 1999
305.896'073'0092—dc21
    [B]   98-8718
                                             CIP
                                             AC

© 1999 by Melissa McDaniel
All rights reserved. Published simultaneously in Canada
Printed in the United States of America
1 2 3 4 5 6 7 8 9 10 R 07 06 05 04 03 02 01 00 99

CONTENTS

CHAPTER ONE

A DEATH IN GHANA

On August 27, 1963, in Accra, the capital of the African nation of Ghana, ninety-five-year-old W. E. B. DuBois slipped quietly into death. DuBois's long life had been filled with extraordinary accomplishments. He had been the first African-American to earn a doctorate from Harvard. He was the founder of urban sociology and an esteemed professor and researcher. He wrote more than twenty books, including five novels, two autobiographies, and a collection of carefully argued, provocative works on race, history, and sociology. He was one of the founders of the National Association for the Advancement of Colored People. He had been the founder, editor, and primary force behind *The Crisis*, the leading black magazine of the 1910s and 1920s. He was the Father of Pan-Africanism, a movement that promoted solidarity among people of African descent.

Above all, DuBois had been a leader in the civil rights movement in America and in the struggle of Africans to free themselves from colonialism. He had worked, studied, written, argued, and provoked long after most people ease into retirement. By all accounts, he was one of the greatest black scholars who had ever lived.

In Ghana, where DuBois was honored for his remarkable achievements, he was given an elaborate state funeral. Every nation with a consulate in Ghana sent a representative to DuBois's funeral. Every nation except one, that is. The United States sent no one to the funeral.

DuBois's politics had become increasingly radical at a time when the United States was becoming increasingly conservative. He was once a leading spokesman for black Americans, but many of his friends and admirers in the United States had abandoned him over time and his government had harassed him. A few months before his death, when the United States refused to renew his passport, DuBois felt morally obliged to renounce his U.S. citizenship. One of the most extraordinary men the United States has ever produced chose to die a Ghanian.

Eight years before his death, DuBois had written a "Last Message to the World," which was read as his coffin was lowered into the African

DuBois was given a state funeral in Ghana, where he
had been revered by powerful political figures and
schoolchildren alike.

soil. DuBois wrote, "I have loved my work, I have loved my people and my play, but always I have been uplifted by the thought that what I have done will live long and justify my life."

> **"I have been uplifted by the thought that what I have done will live long and justify my life."**

That evening, Ghanian president Kwame Nkrumah gave a radio address. After discussing his friend's great life, he concluded, "Dr. DuBois is a phenomenon. May he rest in peace."

CHAPTER 2

A CHILD OF NEW ENGLAND

Ninety-five years earlier, on February 23, 1868, William Edward Burghardt DuBois had been born in Great Barrington, Massachusetts. Great Barrington was a proper New England town of about 5,000 people in the Berkshire Hills in western Massachusetts. Only about fifty of Great Barrington's residents were African-American, but their families had been there for generations, and they were established members of the community.

DuBois's great-great-grandfather, Tom, had been kidnapped in West Africa and brought to America as a slave, where he was given the last name Burghardt. Tom fought in the Revolutionary War (1775–1783) and was freed. Shortly thereafter, all the slaves in Massachusetts were freed.

Tom Burghardt's descendants became farmers, domestic workers, and waiters. By the time Mary Burghardt gave birth to her son, William, less than 100 years later, the Burghardts had long

Childhood home, Great Barrington, Massachusetts. Will lived in a poor neighborhood, but he was accepted by wealthy families due to his intellect and ambition.

been respected members of the Great Barrington community.

The same could not be said of the DuBois side of the family. DuBois's grandfather, Alexander, was the son of a white plantation owner in the Bahamas and a black slave. Alexander and his brother were light-skinned, and their father raised them as his own and sent them to a private school in Connecticut. After their father died, however, their white relatives decided they should be treated as if they were black. Alexander was taken out of school and made an apprentice to a shoemaker.

Alexander was a proud young man, accustomed to the privileges of a white gentleman. He refused to accept his new status and spent the rest of his life trying to recapture what he had

Will's father, Alfred DuBois, served in the Union army.

enjoyed as a child. His various business endeavors required some travel, and for a time he lived in the island nation of Haiti. He married three times. His son, Alfred, was born in Haiti and, like his father, spent much of his time moving around. Alfred DuBois worked as a barber and a cook, fought in the Union Army during the Civil War (1861–1865), roamed throughout the lush valleys of western Massachusetts, and eventually stopped in Great Barrington, where he met Mary Burghardt.

The Burghardts did not approve of this handsome drifter, who had no job, no prospects, and worse yet, no family connections or respectability. Ignoring her family's complaints, Mary ran away and married Alfred in 1867. The following year, William was born.

When William was very young, Alfred left the family to establish himself in Connecticut. He was supposed to send for his wife and son, but he never did, and neither Mary nor William ever saw him again. The Burghardts felt their suspicions of Alfred's character were proved correct. But DuBois always blamed his mother's family for being snobbish and making his father feel unwelcome. "The Burghardts didn't like it, because he was too white," DuBois said much later, "and he had a lot of extra manners which they weren't used to . . . At any rate, they practically drove him away."

With his father gone, William and his mother moved onto her parents' farm. Later in life, DuBois often described his childhood as idyllic. Days were spent exploring the countryside and playing with his many cousins. After Mary's father died, she and William moved into town,

Will DuBois as a young child, age four or five.

where she worked as a domestic servant until she suffered a stroke and was no longer able to work regularly. They "must often have been near the edge of poverty," DuBois wrote later. "Yet I was not hungry or in lack of suitable clothing and shoes, or made to feel unfortunate." After Mary's illness, the close-knit community did what they could to help out. Relatives and neighbors made sure they had enough money to buy shoes and books. William pitched in by earning money delivering groceries, selling newspapers, and mowing lawns.

Despite the hardships they faced, Mary was determined that her son would have a good education. William was always at the top of the class at the local public school, far ahead of even much older children. "Art Benham could draw pictures" better, DuBois remembered later, but he himself "could express meaning in words better." DuBois also recalled, "Mike Gibbons was a perfect marble player, but dumb in Latin."

For much of his youth, DuBois felt little racism around him. By and large, DuBois's friends were his white classmates. He was very popular with his white teachers, and his family was respected. But gradually it dawned on William that the color of his skin set him apart. One day, he and his classmates were exchanging visiting cards. When he offered his card to a white girl new to the school, she refused it. Because of this and other slights, William slowly began to isolate him-

Mary Silvina Burghardt DuBois, Will's mother. Unlike many parents of her day, she did not train her son out of left-handedness.

self. Such insults also made him more determined to succeed and to show the world how wrong racism was.

The Burghardts raised DuBois to value orderliness, neatness, and hard work, for they were very much part of the New England culture around them. In this culture, "Standing did not depend on what the ancestor did, or who he was, but rather that he existed, lived decently and thus linked the individual to the community," DuBois once wrote. The same attitudes that rejected his father as an outsider also meant that African-Americans in Great Barrington were accepted and respected, because of their long standing in the community. The same was not true of the Irish and German immigrants who worked in the town's woolen mills. Young William accepted the values of his community without question and looked down on the millworkers because of their poverty and lack of manners. DuBois later admitted that, like the people around him, "I cordially despised the poor Irish and South Germans." He fully accepted that the world was fair, "that wealth was the result of work and saving and that the rich rightly inherited the earth. The poor, on the whole, were themselves to be blamed."

"I cordially despised the poor Irish and South Germans."

At this time, however, DuBois knew nothing of the ways of the world. He had rarely been outside his small town and knew little of what lay beyond it. Over the years, as he saw more, experienced more, and studied more, he would come to realize that the world was far from just, and that many factors—including race and class discrimination—kept people "in their place."

Entering high school, DuBois devoted himself even more seriously to his studies. He took classes that would prepare him for college, including geometry, algebra, Latin, and Greek. He also haunted a local bookstore owned by a man named Johnny Morgan. Morgan took a liking to the young scholar and let him read the books and magazines there. When William absolutely had to have a set of history books, Morgan let the young man buy them on credit.

Morgan helped William get a job as the Great Barrington correspondent for the *Springfield Republican* newspaper. The teenager also wrote articles for the *New York Globe*, an African-American weekly, urging blacks to take part in the political process. We "hold the balance of power," the sixteen-year-old stated, arguing that if blacks "will only act in concert, they may become a power not to be despised." Already DuBois was becoming conscious of the importance of race. If blacks were to take their rightful place in society, they needed to act as a group.

DuBois graduated at the head of his class in 1884. He was the only black student among the dozen graduates and the first black student ever to graduate from Great Barrington High School. The entire community was proud of the brilliant young scholar. Although few students from Great Barrington, black or white, attended college, DuBois was determined to go, and the townspeople did what they could to support him. A group of prominent men set up a scholarship for him. Meanwhile, he spent the next year studying, working, and saving money for college.

DuBois wanted to attend Harvard, the nation's most prestigious college, which was in Cambridge, Massachusetts. But the tuition there was very expensive, and his high school education was not up to the entrance standards of Harvard. His white backers eventually told him that they had raised enough money for him to attend Fisk, a black university in Nashville, Tennessee.

When DuBois's family heard this recommendation, they were adamantly opposed. His mother did not want her son moving to the South, where slavery was a recent memory and racism was much more overt and violent than it was in the North. William was disappointed—he wanted to attend Harvard, Yale, or some other elite institution—but he put the best face on it. If he was going to be a leader among African-Americans, he

Graduating class of Great Barrington High School, 1884. DuBois is on the far left.

reasoned, he would need to learn more about the South, because that's where most blacks lived.

A few months before he was set to leave, his mother died. Now he really had nothing to keep him in Massachusetts. So he rather naively set off on what he thought would be a great adventure, to "the South of slavery, rebellion, and black folk."

CHAPTER 3

THE YEARS OF PREPARATION

Arriving at Fisk University was a culture shock for the seventeen-year-old W. E. B. DuBois. For the first time, he was immersed in a wholly black world. In Massachusetts, he had often been the only black person in school and in other situations. Now he moved through crowds of black men and women, most of whom were southern and whose parents had been slaves. DuBois loved it. "I was thrilled to be for the first time among so many people of my own color," he wrote. "Never before had I seen young men so self-assured and who gave themselves such airs, and colored men at that."

> **"I was thrilled to be for the first time among so many people of my own color."**

Although he was younger than many of his classmates, his excellent high school education allowed him to begin college as a sophomore. Once again he excelled at his studies, mastering Greek, Latin, French, botany, and calculus. He threw himself into extracurricular activities, writing for and later editing the *Fisk Herald*, the school newspaper. He joined a singing group and organized the financing of a gymnasium.

The world off campus was not so welcoming. In the aftermath of the Civil War, blacks had taken advantage of their newly won civil rights. They voted and were elected to office. They learned new trades and went to college. But the

At seventeen, Will was a socially awkward, impressionable sophomore at Fisk University.

progress Southern society was making did not last long. By the 1880s, traditional conservative Southerners had reasserted their power. Discrimination was legalized. Blacks were not allowed to ride in the same railway cars as whites. They went to separate schools and used separate bathrooms. Gradually, laws were passed that denied most Southern blacks the vote. And more and more blacks were suffering random violence and even murder at the hands of Southern racists.

It was this world that DuBois confronted whenever he left the campus. Insults were common—and shocking. While in town one day he accidentally brushed against a white woman. He raised his hat in apology, but the woman responded with fury and hate. DuBois learned a lesson about society in the South. Black people could not treat whites as if they were equal. DuBois was appalled. Never again would he raise his hat to a Southern white woman.

After his first year of college, DuBois decided to spend the summer teaching in a rural area in order to learn more about the lives and thoughts of Southern blacks. He roamed around eastern Tennessee looking for a school that needed a teacher. Finally he found one near the town of Alexandria. The school was nothing but a small log hut with no windows, no chalkboards, and only a few books.

That summer DuBois learned about the desperate poverty endured by most Southern blacks. He experienced their impossibly hard lives as well as their warmth, dignity, and beauty. His favorite student, Josie, was a young woman of about twenty who had "the shadow of an unconscious moral heroism that would willingly give all of life to make life broader, deeper, and fuller for her and hers." He taught at the same school the following summer and then did not return to Alexandria again for a decade. When he finally visited, he learned that Josie had died, defeated by poverty and hardship.

Will's time in the South exposed him to the poverty of freed slaves.

Three years after leaving Great Barrington, DuBois had learned that the black world was "held back by race prejudice and legal bonds, as well as by deep ignorance and dire poverty." He later wrote, "Into this world I leapt with enthusiasm. A new loyalty and allegiance replaced my Americanism: henceforward I was a Negro."

> **"A new loyalty and allegiance replaced my Americanism: henceforward I was a Negro."**

Although DuBois had earned a bachelors of arts degree at Fisk, his dream of going to Harvard had not waned. He now set his sights on the elite institution with the goal of earning a Ph.D. He was admitted to Harvard, but they required that he begin as a junior and repeat two years of undergraduate study before beginning graduate school, because academic requirements at Fisk were not rigorous enough. Eager to learn and explore, DuBois was happy to comply.

So DuBois headed back north, to the state of his birth. At Harvard, he quickly established himself as a brilliant scholar and earned the friendship and respect of his professors, but he shied away from socializing with his fellow students. Other black students at the school had white friends, but DuBois chose to isolate himself. He lived off campus and devoted his time to study. "Desperately afraid of intruding where I was not wanted," he later explained, he became "encased in a completely colored world." Yet he did join the philosophy club. And because he had always enjoyed singing, he applied to join the Harvard Glee Club, only to be rejected. "I ought to have known," he later wrote, "that Harvard could not afford to have a Negro on its Glee Club traveling about the country."

"I ought to have known that Harvard could not afford to have a Negro on its Glee Club traveling about the country."

Fisk University's thirteenth graduating class, 1888. DuBois, seated at left, gave a commencement address on "Bismark, my hero."

DuBois became active in Boston's black community. He wrote for the *Boston Courant*, a black newspaper, and gave speeches before the National Colored League of Boston criticizing African-American churches for not doing enough to help black communities. He also criticized the black community as a whole for not being sufficiently concerned with intellectual and cultural pursuits. People should establish libraries and reading circles, he argued. To this end, he helped mount a production of *The Birds*, by the classical Greek playwright Aristophanes. "I tried to take culture out into the colored community of Boston," he wrote later.

W. E. B. DuBois distinguished himself academically at Harvard. In 1890, he earned a B.A. in philosophy with honors and was one of six students chosen to speak at the graduation. DuBois seized this as an opportunity to discuss slavery and chose Jefferson Davis, the president of the Confederacy during the Civil War, as the subject of his talk. According to DuBois, Davis represented "the idea of the Strong Man," which turned "a naturally brave and generous man" into the "champion of a people fighting to be free in order that another people shall not be free." DuBois argued that Davis, like all "strong men," was an oppressor. He explained, "His life can only logically mean this: the advance of a part of the world at the expense of the whole; the overweening sense of the 'I' and the consequent forgetting of the

DuBois with his class at Harvard, 1890. Here he received the first failing grade of his life, for an English composition paper.

'Thou.'" DuBois's speech received enthusiastic praise. "DuBois handled his difficult and hazardous subject with absolute good taste, great moderation, and almost contemptuous fairness," commented an observer in the *Nation*.

Now it seemed there was no stopping DuBois. In the next two years, he earned his master's degree from Harvard and was elected to the American Historical Association. His master's thesis, "The Enforcement of the Slave Trade Laws," was published to great acclaim.

DuBois decided to continue his studies in Germany, which at that time boasted the best universities in the world. The problem, of course, was money. He applied for a grant from the John F. Slater Fund for Negro Education. Although he was told that the program had been discontinued, he pursued it so doggedly that they finally gave him a grant anyway. He was "walking on air," after he heard that his studies would be funded, he later recalled. "I saw an especially delectable shirt in a shop window. I went in and asked about it. It cost three dollars, which was about four times as much as I had ever paid for a shirt in my life, but I bought it."

In Germany, DuBois devoted himself, as always, to his studies, absorbing economics, history, and politics, and learning about rigorous scientific research. But he also learned much from the world around him. When not in class, he traveled widely, visiting art museums, attending symphonies, and enjoying the company of his friends. "I became more human," he later said of this period, and "learned the place of 'Wine, Women, and Song.'" Twice he was involved in serious relationships with young women. Although marriage was discussed, he dismissed the idea because the prospect of living as an interracial couple in America was too overwhelming.

The two years DuBois spent in Europe altered his life and his outlook. He learned that oppression was not merely a matter of black and white. While color prejudice was much less common there, hatreds raged over nationality, religion, and ethnicity. The discrimination Jews faced in Germany was sadly familiar to him, and the serfs in Eastern Europe lived in deeper poverty than African-Americans in the rural American South. Gradually, he was developing a broader view of oppression.

Living in a society where blacks were considered regular people rather than outcasts also changed his attitudes on race relations and prejudice. The Europeans he met treated him as an equal, and he in turn came to trust them. "Slowly they became, not white folks, but folks," he wrote. "I ceased to hate or suspect people simply because they belonged to one race or color." After two years in Europe, he had more hope. He said, "I felt myself standing, not against the world, but simply against American narrowness and color prejudice, with the greater, finer world at my back urging me on."

"Slowly they became, not white folks, but folks."

In June 1894, DuBois sailed back home to America an extraordinarily well-educated young man. He later wrote, "The years of preparation were over and life was to begin."

CHAPTER 4

BUILDING A CAREER

When W. E. B. DuBois arrived in New York, he had only enough money in his pocket for a train ticket to Great Barrington with two dollars to spare. Needing a job, he wrote to black colleges seeking a teaching position. Although he was most interested in sociology and history, he was too desperate to be picky.

The first offer he received was from Wilberforce University in central Ohio. They would pay $800 a year for a Greek and Latin teacher. DuBois immediately accepted.

DuBois and Wilberforce were quite a shock to each other. In his time abroad, DuBois had transformed himself into a European gentleman. He arrived at the small college wearing gloves and a tall silk hat and carrying a cane. But it was more than his clothes that set him apart. DuBois was outspoken and strong-minded, and he had high expectations of what a university should be. He was, he later admitted, "cocky and self-satisfied."

Wilberforce, which was run by the African Methodist Episcopal Church, was a deeply religious institution. Church services were compulsory and religious revivals on campus were common. During these times, DuBois locked himself in his room and passed the time studying, trying to ignore the emotional upheavals outside. His annoyance with the school's intense religiosity almost cost him his job. Once he entered a room where a prayer meeting was being held. A student said, "Professor DuBois will lead us in prayer." "No, he won't," DuBois snapped back. DuBois had some difficulty explaining his actions to the school's governing board. Luckily, the university recognized that DuBois was a brilliant scholar and didn't dismiss him.

DuBois's impatience with Wilberforce's religious fervor isolated him. But he took advantage of his spare time to work on his doctoral dissertation, "The Suppression of the African Trade to the United States of America, 1638–1870." In 1895, when his dissertation was approved, he became the first African-American to earn a Ph.D. from Harvard.

That following year, DuBois was offered a position at the University of Pennsylvania. DuBois happily accepted. Soon he and his new

*Nina Gomer DuBois, often refered to simply as "wife,"
had been DuBois's student.*

bride, Nina Gomer, who had been a student at
Wilberforce, settled down in a black ghetto in
Philadelphia.

DuBois undertook his job—to research the
social conditions of blacks in the city's Seventh
Ward—with great enthusiasm. He was convinced that ignorance was at the root of discrimi-

nation, and that as soon as scientific research proved that white fears of blacks were unfounded, prejudice would dissipate. "The world was thinking wrong about race, because it did not know," he said. "The cure for it was knowledge based on scientific investigation."

DuBois did all of that investigation himself. During the next year, he

"The world was thinking wrong about race, because it did not know."

personally interviewed thousands of people. Methodically, he moved from house to house, door to door, asking people about their jobs, schooling, and families. After a year of round-the-clock work, he had accumulated a mountain of information, which he eventually put into a book called *The Philadelphia Negro*.

At this time, whites tended to view all blacks as the same. One of DuBois's most important conclusions was that this was wrong. There was, in fact, a class structure within the black community that ranged from middle class to working class to poor to criminal. DuBois concluded that whites only paid attention to the criminal class, and did little to provide opportunity or rewards for working- or middle-class people. He further concluded that many blacks were being held back by discrimination.

The Philadelphia Negro was a landmark in urban sociology. Never before had anyone system-

The Philadelphia slums where Will and Nina first made their home.

atically studied blacks in America. DuBois's methods of gathering and analyzing social information would be employed time and again in the future.

For DuBois, this was only the beginning. He realized that much more needed to be learned about the lives of African-Americans. The opportunity for him to do further research arose when he was offered a position as professor of history and economics at Atlanta University, a black college in Georgia. DuBois was thrilled, and he, Nina, and their newborn son, Burghardt, moved south.

In Atlanta, DuBois was assigned to direct a conference on urban African-American life. He used the conference as a platform to initiate an ambitious program to study black America. Each year for ten years, the conference would study a different aspect of black life, including business, education, labor, and crime. According to DuBois's plan, at the end of the ten years, the subjects would be repeated during another ten-year cycle and so on for 100 years. Over the course of a century, they would compile a tremendous research base about African-American society. This knowledge, DuBois believed, would inevitably change the attitudes of white people. "The ultimate evil was stupidity," he said, which could be cured by "carefully gathered scientific proof that neither color nor race determined the limits of a man's capacity."

> **"The ultimate evil was stupidity."**

At this time, almost all of what passed as scholarly works about African-Americans were nothing more than racist essays. While the authors of such works spouted hatred without any research or study, DuBois's Atlanta publications were careful scientific studies based upon statistical research and interviews. The publications were virtually the only information available about black life, and they received high praise from many scholars and newspapers.

DuBois was happy at Atlanta University, where he made many enduring friendships, but he rarely left campus. In the outside world, life for African-Americans was getting worse. Jim Crow laws, which mandated that the races be separated, had become the norm. In Atlanta, streetcars, elevators, and even parks were segregated. Most blacks were unable to vote, and the number of blacks who were being lynched was increasing.

The idiocy of the Jim Crow laws infuriated DuBois. Later, he wrote about climbing into a run-down railroad car "caked with dirt" that was

Jim Crow laws persisted for more than a century throughout the South.

reserved for blacks. "The floor [was] . . . gummy and the windows dirty." DuBois wrote that on the trains, "It is difficult to get lunch or drinking water. Lunch rooms either 'don't serve niggers' or serve them at some dirty and ill-attended hole in the wall . . . . If you have to change cars be wary of junctions which are usually without accommodation and filled with quarrelsome whites who hate a 'darky' dressed up."

In 1899, DuBois's two-year-old son Burghardt died of diphtheria. The child had contracted the disease from the city's water, which had been tainted by sewage. The DuBoises were devastated by this loss. "The child's death tore our lives in two," he later wrote. "I threw myself more completely into my work, while most reason for living left the soul of my wife." Although another child, Yolande, was born the following year, Nina never really recovered from Burghardt's death.

"The child's death tore our lives in two."

Meanwhile, DuBois's scholarly achievements and writings were bringing him increasing prominence. In 1900, he was invited to create an exhibit on black American life for a world's fair being held in Paris. The collection of photographs, maps, books, and plans that DuBois put together so impressed the judges that they awarded him a gold medal.

The young couple with son Burghardt in 1897.
The child died two years later.

DuBois was a renowned scholar by this time. But he had discovered that scientific language was not always the most effective means of expression. In 1903, he published a collection of essays called *The Souls of Black Folk*, a book written with such grace that it has become a classic and is as resonant today as it was a hundred years ago. In the book, DuBois expressed the paradoxes of being an African-American— of being both black and American. African-Americans, DuBois explained, always filtered their self-image through the eyes of whites. He wrote, "It is a peculiar sensation, this double-consciousness, this sense of always looking at one's self through the eyes of others, of measuring one's soul by the tape of a world that looks on in amused contempt and pity. One ever feels his twoness,—an American, a Negro; two souls, two thoughts, two unreconciled strivings; two warring ideals in one dark body, whose dogged strength alone keeps it from being torn asunder."

Many of the essays in *The Souls of Black Folk* had originally appeared in such magazines as *Atlantic* and *The New York Times Magazine*. But the one that garnered the most attention, entitled "Of Mr. Booker T. Washington and Others," was written specially for the book. In this essay, DuBois directly questioned the wisdom of the man who was generally considered the spokesman for African-Americans. Having established himself as a leading scholar, DuBois was now ready to challenge Booker T. Washington for the role of spokesman.

CHAPTER 5

A BATTLE FOR LEADERSHIP

Booker T. Washington could not have had a more different background from that of W. E. B. DuBois. Washington was a Southerner rather than a Northerner. He had been born a slave in Virginia in 1856. Slaves received no education, but Washington managed to teach himself to read. After the Civil War, when the slaves were freed, he labored in the coal mines of West Virginia. Later, he worked as a janitor at the Hampton Institute, a black school in Virginia, where he also took classes. By age twenty, he was teaching at Hampton.

Washington had seen and experienced the struggles of former slaves firsthand. Many had neither a source of income nor any prospect of one. Washington believed that African-Americans needed to be taught skills that would enable them to make a living. Higher education could wait,

Washington thought, until the economic needs of everyday life were taken care of.

Booker T. Washington put these ideas into action at the Tuskegee Institute in Alabama. When the Alabama legislature had established Tuskegee as a school for blacks, it had agreed to pay teachers but had offered no money for buildings, books, or other resources. So Washington and his students built the school themselves. At Tuskegee, Washington preached the importance of hard work, self-reliance, and learning a useful trade. The school soon blossomed. By 1900, 1,000 students attended Tuskegee.

To build and promote the school, Washington had learned how to get along with whites. He was adept at convincing wealthy whites that funding his school—and creating skilled workers—was in their interest.

Washington was generally considered the spokesman for black America. He had been catapulted into this role after a speech he made in 1895 at the Cotton States and International Exposition in Atlanta. "The wisest among my race understand that the agitation of questions of social equality is the extremest folly," Washington said. Instead, he argued, blacks should focus on improving their work skills and contributing to the economy. Washington continued, "In all things that are purely social we can be as separate as the

Booker T. Washington in 1903. His nondemanding approach to civil rights issues put him at odds with DuBois.

fingers, yet one as the hand in all things essential to mutual progress." Washington appeared to be accepting segregation in return for economic development among African-Americans. "The opportunity to earn a dollar in a factory just now is worth infinitely more than the opportunity to spend a dollar in an opera house." This speech became known as the Atlanta Compromise address.

Not surprisingly, white people across the country hailed Washington's stance as wise and prudent. President Grover Cleveland sent him a letter of congratulations. A few black leaders were disturbed by the speech. John Hope, who would later become president of Atlanta University, wrote, "If we are not striving for equality, in heaven's name for what are we living?" Many other blacks, however, felt that the Atlanta Compromise was a reasonable starting point. Even DuBois praised the speech, saying "It might be the basis of a real settlement between whites and blacks in the South."

At first, DuBois admired Washington's emphasis on self-reliance and personal responsibility. But gradually, he came to believe that Washington's conciliatory talk was counterproductive. He was irritated by Washington's unwillingness to stand up for black voting rights and by his persistent call for vocational, rather than academic, education for blacks. For DuBois, progress required more than work skills. "It wasn't enough to teach Negroes trades," he once said. "The Negro had to have some voice in their government, they had to have protection in the courts, and they had to have trained men to lead them."

DuBois argued that an educated black elite—what he called the Talented Tenth, because it comprised about 10 percent of the African-American population—was needed to lead the race into freedom and full participation in American life. Blacks could not simply follow whites, as Washington seemed to be suggesting. That would make them forever second-class citizens. "The Negro race, like all races, is going to be saved by its exceptional men," DuBois said. "Was there ever a nation on God's fair earth civilized from the bottom upward? Never; it is, ever was, and ever will be from the top downward that culture filters."

> **"The Negro race, like all races, is going to be saved by its exceptional men."**

By the time DuBois wrote "Of Mr. Booker T. Washington and Others" for *The Souls of Black Folk*, he had come to believe that Washington's ideas were thoroughly wrongheaded. Washington's accommodationist policy "practically accepts the alleged inferiority of the Negro races," he said. DuBois argued that civil rights and racial self-respect were more important than material possessions, and that African-Americans must demand proper treatment. Throughout history, he explained, "the doctrine preached has been that manly self-respect is worth more than lands and houses . . . . [and] that a people who surrender voluntarily such respect, or cease striving for it, are not worth civilizing."

While Washington argued that blacks had to prove themselves worthy of equality, DuBois maintained that racism was the root of the problem. "Relentless color-prejudice is more often a cause than a result of the Negro's degradation," he wrote.

By the turn of the century, it had become apparent that Washington's accommodationist policies were not doing blacks any good. Racial violence was rampant, segregation was increasing, and black voting rights were being taken away. In Louisiana in 1896, there had been more than 130,000 registered black voters. In 1900, there were only about 5,000. In Alabama in 1900, only about 3,000 black men were registered out of more than 180,000 black men of voting age.

As the racial situation deteriorated, criticism of Washington by DuBois and others had grown louder. But Washington had tremendous power, and he tried to silence those who disagreed with him. Washington had the support of congressmen, business leaders, and philanthropists, who looked to him as the voice of black America. They followed his advice when it came to lending their name or money to causes or institutions.

Washington also had a network of African-Americans throughout the country who did his bidding. He used them to suppress other points of view. Only people who agreed with his ideas would have their programs funded or their articles printed in newspapers. Washington's network of associates came to be called the "Tuskegee machine." According to DuBois, "Few political appointments of Negroes were made in the United States without his consent. Even the careers of rising young colored men were very often determined by his advice and certainly his opposition was fatal."

But some of Washington's opponents, particularly those who ran independent newspapers, could not be silenced. William Monroe Trotter, the editor of the *Boston Guardian*, was among Washington's loudest critics. Another was Ida B. Wells-Barnett, a passionate journalist and anti-lynching activist. But gradually, the voice of the reserved intellectual at Atlanta University rose above the others. W. E. B. DuBois was being forced to take a more public stand.

At Atlanta University, DuBois tried to remove himself from the vicious world outside. Horrified at the state of race relations and finding the indignities of Jim Crow practices unbearable, he rarely left campus. But given the increasing violence against blacks, DuBois was finding he could no longer remain isolated in the world of academia.

In 1903, an African-American named Sam Hose was arrested for murder. DuBois knew that the man was likely to be lynched. Thinking a reasoned argument might prevent the lynching, he wrote a statement to take to the *Atlanta Consti-*

*Ida Wells-Barnett was a settlement house pioneer
who spoke out against the Atlanta Compromise.*

tution. On the way to the newspaper office, he
learned that he was too late, that Hose had
already been killed. "They said his knuckles were
on exhibition at a grocery store farther down on
Mitchell Street, along which I was walking,"
DuBois later recalled. "I turned back to the university."

DuBois had always believed that his work as scholar and educator could make him a leader among African-Americans and that education could end the race problem. But this seemed less and less true. His sensible arguments and presentation of the facts had done Sam Hose no good. How could they really be expected to prevent such obscene violence and hatred? DuBois was realizing that he was going to have to become a more active and vocal leader. "I began to turn aside from my [scholarly] work," he wrote.

That same year, following DuBois's criticism of Washington in *The Souls of Black Folk*, articles appeared in the black press reprimanding DuBois for daring to question Washington. But things remained fairly quiet until July, when William Monroe Trotter and others disrupted a speech Washington was giving in Boston. Trotter was arrested and spent a month in jail.

DuBois criticized Trotter's actions, but he also stated that he thought the jail term was unreasonable. Later that year, he stayed at Trotter's home when visiting Boston. Though DuBois had no prior knowledge of Trotter's plans and was not even in Boston at the time, Washington began spreading the word that DuBois had been behind the disruption. DuBois was not behaving as Washington wanted him to behave, so the Tuskegee machine kicked into action to punish him. Benefactors of Atlanta University were told to stop making donations to the college, and the university's president was told to get DuBois into line.

But instead of intimidating DuBois, such attacks only pushed him to a more radical position, and he became more outspoken in disparaging Washington's policies. Still, it wasn't until 1905 that DuBois openly attacked Washington and the Tuskegee machine. He accused Washington of giving newspapers money to print what he wanted them to print. Washington scoffed at these charges, as did many black papers that supported him. The *New York Age* dubbed DuBois the "Professor of hysterics." Others demanded proof. It does appear that Washington tried to funnel

"Professor of hysterics."

money to newspapers that supported him and to drive those who disagreed with him out of business. DuBois was certain that Washington used bribery and threats to get his way. He insisted that Washington "was seeking not the welfare of the Negro race but personal power."

DuBois had decided that it was no longer possible to work with Washington. New leadership was needed in black America. Now was the time for action.

CHAPTER 6

A MASTER OF PROPAGANDA

W. E. B. DuBois decided to organize a group of African-American leaders, who would operate completely independently of Booker T. Washington. In June 1905, he sent out a call "for organized determination and aggressive action on the part of men who believe in Negro freedom and growth." He invited a select group of people to a meeting in Fort Erie, Canada, near Niagara Falls, to discuss a new approach to improving conditions for African-Americans. No one with any connection to the Tuskegee machine was invited.

Although Washington found out about the conference and succeeded in pressuring a few people into staying home, twenty-nine influential blacks from fourteen states showed up. This was the beginning of the Niagara Movement, a group that demanded civil rights and equality for black Americans. They pushed for the vote for all men, freedom of speech and press, and the elimination

The first meeting of the Niagara Movement, 1905.
Women were voted in as members the following year.

of distinctions based on color. The movement
called for federal laws to override the unjust Jim
Crow laws passed by state governments. They
also called for "persistent manly agitation" as a
better approach than Washington's "cowardice
and apology."

Although the Niagara Movement was tiny, Washington viewed it as competition and did his best to destroy it. He tried to prevent the press from covering the meeting. The following year, when the movement held its second conference in Harpers Ferry, West Virginia, some of Washington's supporters secretly attended the meetings so they could report back to him. Washington pressured federal officials into dismissing members of the Niagara Movement who worked for the government. He also claimed that DuBois was simply trying to usurp his leadership and gain power for himself.

Although Washington was unable to destroy the Niagara Movement, it was destined to remain small. To a certain extent, DuBois blamed himself for this, because he considered himself too reserved and acerbic to head a popular movement. "I was no natural leader of men," he once admitted. "I could not slap people on the back and make friends of strangers." DuBois's colleague William H. Ferris once noted that "DuBois is gifted with a more powerful intellect than Washington, is a more uncompromising idealist, and is a more brilliant writer . . . . But Washington is a more magnetic speaker and more astute politician, a greater humorist, and less of an aristocrat."

The Niagara Movement limped along for only a few years, but it did provide an alternative to Washington's apologetic approach. The movement

issued a statement that said, "We claim for our-
selves every single right that belongs to a freeborn
American, political, civil, and social; and until we
get these rights we will never cease to protest and
assail the ears of America."

In 1906, a riot erupted in Atlanta. Whites
rampaged through the streets, beating blacks at
random. Ten people were killed. Then in 1908, a
race riot swept through Springfield, Illinois. The
symbolism of racial violence in the hometown of

*The Niagara Movement in 1907. DuBois is
seated to the left.*

Abraham Lincoln, the man who had issued the Emancipation Proclamation freeing the slaves, disturbed many people. Many Northern whites were outraged and feared that the racial violence of the South would engulf the North. The need to protest and the failure of Washington's policies were patently obvious. "We must come to treat the Negro on a plane of absolute political and social equality," wrote white journalist William English Walling, "or [white supremacists] will soon have transferred the Race War to the North."

Liberal Northern whites agreed. Some, including Mary Ovington, a social reformer, and Oswald Garrison Villard, editor of the *New York Evening Post*, created the National Negro Committee to try to chart a new course for black advancement. Many black leaders refused to attend the meeting, which was dominated by whites. But DuBois thought the opportunity to influence prominent whites was too valuable to pass up. He presented a careful critique of Washington's approach that was well received.

The following year, in 1910, a permanent organization was established called the National Association for the Advancement of Colored People (NAACP), which would become the most prominent civil rights organization of the twentieth century. Initially, the organization was made up primarily of whites. In May 1910, at the NAACP's first conference, DuBois was the only black person elected an officer—the director of publicity and research. Still, all but the most radical members of the Niagara Movement joined the NAACP.

DuBois was finally leaving academia and becoming a popular leader of black Americans. After thirteen years in Atlanta, he headed north to New York City. "My career as a scientist," DuBois later said, "was to be swallowed up in my role as master of propaganda."

DuBois's primary task as the NAACP's director of publicity and research was to establish and edit a monthly journal for black America, which he called *The Crisis*. DuBois envisioned *The Crisis* as a both a newspaper to report "important happenings and movements in the world which bear on the great problem of interracial relations" and as a forum for swaying opinion and pushing for action. "Its editorial page will stand for the rights of men, irrespective of color or race, for the highest ideals of American democracy, and for reasonable but earnest and persistent attempts to gain these rights and realize these ideals," he wrote.

This was not the first time DuBois had founded a newspaper. In 1905, he published a short-lived weekly called the *Moon*. Then in 1907, he founded a monthly called the *Horizon*, which lasted for about three years. DuBois had also written for popular magazines such as the *Nation* and *Collier's*.

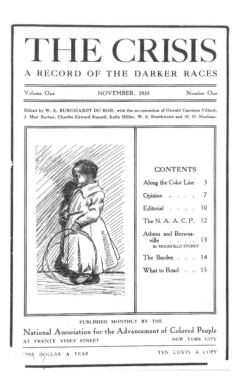

THE CRISIS

A RECORD OF THE DARKER RACES

Volume One   NOVEMBER, 1910   Number One

Edited by W. E. BURGHARDT DU BOIS, with the co-operation of Oswald Garrison Villard,
J. Max Barber, Charles Edward Russell, Kelly Miller, W. S. Braithwaite and M. D. Maclean.

CONTENTS

Along the Color Line   3

Opinion   7

Editorial   10

The N. A. A. C. P.   12

Athens and Browns-
ville   13
By MOORFIELD STOREY

The Burden . . .   14

What to Read . .   15

PUBLISHED MONTHLY BY THE
National Association for the Advancement of Colored People
AT TWENTY VESEY STREET   NEW YORK CITY

ONE DOLLAR A YEAR   TEN CENTS A COPY

*First issue of The Crisis, edited by DuBois
for twenty-four years.*

But DuBois had never before had such a regular forum for his opinions. Although *The Crisis* was published by the NAACP, DuBois was its independent editor. He wrote what he believed, which did not always reflect the position of the organization.

At *The Crisis*, DuBois had free rein to discuss a wide range of issues. He wrote about history and women's rights, churches and schools, music and art. The magazine also included suggested readings, a section on Talented Tenth firsts, and listings of African-Americans who had been lynched. And constantly, it agitated for change and social equality.

DuBois turned *The Crisis* into the most significant paper in black America. Never before had a black magazine been so aggressive. "We have crawled and pleaded for justice and we have been cheerfully spat upon and murdered and burned," DuBois wrote in 1911, while arguing that blacks should arm themselves during racial attacks. "If we are to die, in God's name let us perish like men and not like bales of hay."

"If we are to die, in God's name let us perish like men and not like bales of hay."

Nor had any black magazine ever been so popular. One thousand copies of the first issue of *The Crisis* were printed. Within three years, its circulation had jumped to 30,000. At its peak, 100,000 people subscribed. It brought news and hope and pride to black families

"I didn't know where the Bible was in the house but I knew where *The Crisis* was."

across America. "We had a big stack of them," recalled one man. "I didn't know where the Bible was in the house but I knew where *The Crisis* was."

The NAACP and DuBois agreed from the beginning that *The Crisis* should not devote much space to attacking Booker T. Washington. But this did not stop Washington from taking on the magazine and the organization. The NAACP's sole purpose is "tearing down our work wherever possible," Washington said. "None of our friends should give it comfort." But Washington's power was waning, and his philosophy had lost credibility. Even before Washington died in 1915, DuBois had become the most significant black leader in the nation.

When World War I (1914–1918) broke out in Europe, DuBois argued that the United States should not become involved. He saw the war as a struggle between European empires, which had casually and brutally divided up much of Africa and Asia, turning them into colonies and sucking out their wealth. DuBois argued that if the European powers were weakened by the war, some oppressed nations might be able to throw off the yoke of colonialism. "Out of this war," he wrote, "will rise, soon or late, an independent China, a self-governing India, an Egypt with representative institutions, an Africa for the Africans, and not merely for business exploitation."

The United States entered the war in 1917. To a certain extent, DuBois believed President Woodrow Wilson's claim that the war would give small nations the right of self-determination. DuBois also concluded that fighting in the war might help African-Americans in their struggle for civil rights. In a column called "Close Ranks," DuBois wrote, "Let us, while this war lasts, forget our special grievances and close ranks shoulder to shoulder with our fellow citizens and the allied nations that are fighting for democracy." Basically, DuBois was arguing that if blacks set aside civil rights questions for the duration of the war and proved themselves loyal soldiers, they would be rewarded when peace returned. Whites would have no choice but to acknowledge the contributions blacks had made in the fight for democracy.

Many *The Crisis* readers were outraged by DuBois's seeming accommodationism. African-American soldiers would be fighting in a segregated army for a country that consistently belittled them. Byron Gunner, a veteran of the Niagara Movement, said that this was "the most opportune time for us to push and keep our 'special grievances' to the fore."

In 1919, the year after the war ended, racial violence swept across the United States. Twenty-six cities were shaken by major race riots. Black soldiers who had served courageously in Europe—

The Silent Protest Parade down Fifth Avenue,
New York City, 1917. The NAACP sponsored the
event to decry mob violence and lynching.
DuBois is third from left, front row.

where they were treated well and were not sub-
jected to the indignities of segregation—had
returned to an America that ignored their patrio-
tism and where segregation was still entrenched.
In this instance, DuBois was proven terribly wrong.

CHAPTER 7

THE FATHER OF PAN-AFRICANISM

After World War I drew to a close in 1918, W. E. B. DuBois joined diplomats and journalists from around the world as they converged on Paris for a peace conference to settle the questions raised by the war. DuBois attended as a representative of the NAACP, hoping to advance the cause of independence for African nations. In this, he was disappointed.

In Paris right after the peace conference, DuBois organized the first Pan-African Congress, which attracted delegates from fifteen countries. DuBois had concluded that racism in the United States and colonialism worldwide were connected. He believed that racial problems in the United States could not be solved without solving racial problems on a global basis. To this end, he worked for self-rule for African and Caribbean nations.

DuBois had been one of the first people to promote the idea of unity among people of African descent around the world. In 1900, he had formed the Pan-African Association. Although the group lasted just two years, it earned him the name "the Father of Pan-Africanism." In the intervening years, DuBois had remained interested in Africa. He presented news about Africa in *The Crisis* and had begun planning an *Encyclopedia Africana*, which would cover the history and current conditions of blacks worldwide.

In Paris, the Pan-African Congress called for more humane and democratic government in Africa, rather than an immediate end to colonialism. Africans should "participate in the government as fast as their development permits," the congress resolved. Although these demands were quite moderate, the organization seemed dangerous to many European and American leaders.

Back in the United States, another kind of Pan-Africanism was growing. A black nationalist from Jamaica named Marcus Garvey was leading a movement that advocated black separatism. Garvey promoted the idea that blacks should be separate from whites in all things and that they should control Africa. Garvey recommended that blacks scattered throughout the world should return to Africa.

Garvey was a dynamic speaker and captivating public figure. Decked out in a bright blue uniform and a plumed hat, he led thousands of followers on parades through Harlem, a black district of New York City. These spectacles filled onlookers with pride. Garvey had such charisma that he soon rivaled DuBois as the leading black American spokesman. His emotional appeal spoke

Jamaican Black Nationalist leader Marcus Garvey, New York, 1922.

to men and women who had never been touched by DuBois's intellectual rhetoric.

Although DuBois thought Garvey's ideas and methods "bombastic, wasteful, illogical and almost illegal," he did his best to ignore Garvey and his movement. But he was concerned that Garvey's ideas would be confused with his own, more rational Pan-African movement.

Garvey, however, had no qualms about attacking DuBois. After the Pan-African Congress, he denounced DuBois as a "reactionary under [the] pay of white men." He accused DuBois of being too close to whites. "You cannot advocate 'close ranks' today and talk 'dark water' tomorrow," Garvey said of DuBois. "You must be 100 percent Negro."

"You must be 100 percent Negro."

DuBois was stunned by the success of Garvey's movement, but he stayed quiet until Garvey formed an alliance with the Ku Klux Klan, a white racist organization that was waging a campaign of terror against blacks, Jews, and Catholics all across the United States. Garvey made the bizarre claim that the Klan's open hatred of blacks made them "better friends" to black people than the NAACP, which hoped to bring blacks and whites closer together.

Now that Garvey had formed an "unholy alliance" with the Klan, DuBois could no longer remain silent. In an unusual display, DuBois resorted to insults. He wrote that Garvey was "a liar and a blatant fool," and "a little, fat Black man, ugly, but with intelligent eyes and big head." Garvey shot back that DuBois hated "the

A Ku Klux Klan demonstration in downtown Binghamton, New York, 1924.

black blood in his veins. . . . That is why he likes to dance with white people, and dine with them." He also said that DuBois's education "fits him for no better service than being a lackey for good white people." As the exchange heated up, DuBois received death threats from some Garvey supporters.

In 1924, DuBois wrote, "Marcus Garvey is, without a doubt, the most dangerous enemy of the Negro race in America and in the world. He is either a lunatic or a traitor . . . . This open ally of the Ku Klux Klan should be locked up or sent home." He soon got his wish, when Garvey was arrested for financial misdealings. He was convicted, and in 1927, after two years in prison, Marcus Garvey was deported to Jamaica.

The racial pride evident in Garvey's movement had become common elsewhere. Throughout the African-American community in the 1920s, the arts flourished in what became known as the Harlem Renaissance. Writers such as Langston Hughes, Countee Cullen, and Claude McKay explored issues and images that concerned the African-American community, and jazz was in the air everywhere.

The Crisis played an important role in the Harlem Renaissance. African images graced its cover, and the poetry and stories in it expressed racial pride. DuBois also tried to foster pride among black children by founding a children's magazine called *Brownie's Book*. The magazine included stories about black achievements, legends and poems from around the world, and a column by DuBois in which he spoke in the voice of a character called the Crow. The Crow taught black children that they were beautiful. "I like my black feathers—don't you?" he said.

When the stock market crashed in 1929, the optimism of the Harlem Renaissance crashed with it. The Great Depression began. Unemployment was rampant, reaching fifty percent among blacks. Soup kitchens and breadlines were a common sight.

The Great Depression altered DuBois's program for racial self-development. He became more concerned with the participation of black people in the economy. In 1926, he had traveled to Russia and had been greatly impressed. Although he was not a communist, he admired what communism had achieved in the Soviet Union. Now that the United States was facing widespread poverty and suffering, he advocated some form of "socialization of wealth." In 1934, DuBois suggested in the pages of *The Crisis* that African-Americans needed to form their own economic cooperatives to deal with black poverty. This voluntary segregation, DuBois argued, was different from the racist segregation in public places and schools.

During the Depression in the early 1930s, people out of work sold apples to create income.

DuBois's growing radicalism had long alarmed members of the NAACP board, but this was beyond the pale. Opposition to segregation was a fundamental principle of the NAACP. Walter White, the organization's executive secretary, who did not get along with DuBois, was particularly upset. He reprimanded DuBois for printing opinions contrary to those of the NAACP.

For much of the existence of *The Crisis*, the magazine had been more important than the NAACP, and DuBois had been able to run it independently. But the magazine's circulation had been dropping since the early 1920s, and it had been losing revenue since the late 1920s. Mary Ovington, one of the NAACP's founders and a longtime DuBois ally, told him that now that the NAACP had to give financial support to the magazine, "*The Crisis* would either disappear or become distinctly an NAACP organ, and that means it must be under the [NAACP] secretary."

In May 1934, the NAACP board voted that *The Crisis* could not criticize the association. DuBois immediately resigned. He refused to

"It was like giving up a child."

work without the freedom to speak his mind. Although he felt he had no choice, leaving *The Crisis* was a sad day for DuBois, who had shepherded it through its twenty-four years of existence. He later wrote that leaving *The Crisis* "was like giving up a child."

Although DuBois was sixty-six years old, he was far from ready to retire. He had a standing job offer from his friend John Hope, the president of Atlanta University. DuBois agreed to return to the university on condition that the position be for life.

He didn't want to find himself out in the cold once again. Hope agreed, and DuBois prepared to return south. Nina, however, was not happy about the prospect of returning to a city that held such painful memories. She decided instead to live with their daughter, Yolande, in Baltimore, Maryland.

DuBois returned to the academic life with great gusto. He was a demanding teacher, whose towering and wide-ranging intellect could be intimidating. But for those who got to know him, he was also charming. He returned to his research and founded a social science journal called *Phylon*. He also wrote several important books, including *Black Reconstruction in America: 1860–1880*, which displayed his increasing interest in socialism and class analysis. In Atlanta, DuBois continued to support cooperation as the way to advancement. After another trip to the Soviet Union in 1936, he wrote, "The only hope of humanity today lies in . . . the common interests of the working class."

Although DuBois was still working at an astonishing rate, his influence had waned. Younger black leaders, such as union leader A. Philip Randolph, the founder of the Brotherhood of Sleeping Car Porters, had become more prominent.

As the years wore on, DuBois's radical ideas made some people in Atlanta nervous. Fearing that DuBois might cost the university funding, they urged that he be forced into retirement. John

Hope had died in 1936. So in 1943, the university's board of trustees used the school's mandatory retirement clause as an excuse to force DuBois out. "Without a word of warning I found myself at the age of 76 without employment and with less than $5,000 of savings," DuBois later wrote.

Although he received job offers from several black universities, he chose instead to accept a surprising offer from Walter White at the NAACP to become director of special research. DuBois later surmised that the NAACP had invited him back because they assumed "my life work was done" and that "what I wanted was leisure and comfort and for that I would willingly act as window dressing, say a proper word now and then and give the Association and its secretary moral support."

But the old man still had a lot of fire in him. He was not content to be a mere symbol. In 1945, he was a consultant to the U.S. delegation at the founding of the United Nations, where he argued for an end to colonialism. That same year he participated in the fifth Pan-African Congress in Manchester, England, where he received the respect he deserved as the originator of the movement.

Before long, DuBois and White were again at odds. As he had years before, DuBois expected to be able to act independently. But White did not like some of DuBois's activities, particularly those that seemed to promote socialism. DuBois, meanwhile, did not agree with White's support of President Harry Truman, who was running for reelection. Instead, DuBois supported Henry Wallace of the Progressive Party, which was in favor of important civil rights reforms, and refused to participate in the anticommunist fervor that was sweeping the nation.

The NAACP had a nonpartisan policy. Individuals were not allowed to speak on behalf of candidates or endorse them. But DuBois had no intention of submerging his personal beliefs. He let his name be used on Wallace campaign materials, and he wore a Wallace button around the office. When asked to take the button off, he refused.

In September 1948, DuBois wrote a memo requesting to know exactly what his responsibilities were at the NAACP and complaining about the association's support of Truman's "reactionary, warmongering colonial imperialism." Someone leaked the memo to *The New York Times*. Although DuBois was not responsible for the leak, he was fired.

At eighty years old, W. E. B. DuBois was again out of a job.

CHAPTER 8

THE FINAL YEARS

In 1958, at the age of ninety, W. E. B. DuBois wrote, "I would have been hailed with approval if I had died at 50. At 75 my death was practically requested." As the decades passed, DuBois found himself frequently at odds with prevailing trends. He was becoming more radical as the official policies of the United States were becoming more conservative.

> **"My death was practically requested."**

Following World War II (1939–1945), officials in the United States concluded that communism posed a grave threat to the nation's security. Although the Soviet Union and the United States had been allies during the war, their relationship cooled immediately after the conflict. The Cold War began.

In this tense atmosphere, the U.S. government perceived a communist threat in the government and in society. In the U.S. House of Representatives, the House Un-American Activities Committee began investigating anyone they suspected of being a communist. They pried into people's private lives, asking about their politics and activities, and demanding that they name other people who might be communists. The communist witch-hunt was on.

But a few people had come out of World War II with different ideas. The horrors of the war had convinced them that nothing was more important than peace. Never again should cities be destroyed by a single atomic bomb, as Hiroshima and Nagasaki, Japan, had been. Never again should the world have to experience atrocities like the Nazi concentration camps. To avoid such outrages, nations across the globe would have to work together. To these pacifists, the Cold War was dangerous and could easily erupt into a real war. Because people involved in the peace movement did not join in the anticommunist campaign, they were labeled subversive and were subject to harassment by the U.S. government.

After he was fired from the NAACP, DuBois began working with the Council on African Affairs, an African nationalist group, knowing full well that the U.S. government considered the organization subversive. Similarly, as he became more and more involved in the peace movement, he knew he was being branded a communist sympathizer.

In 1950, DuBois became chairman of the Peace Information Center. The purpose of this organization was to gather signatures for the Stockholm Peace Petition in support of a nuclear-weapons ban. The center also published a newsletter informing Americans about what people in other countries were doing for peace.

That same year, the American Labor Party asked DuBois to run for the U.S. Senate. Although he knew he could not win, he thought his candidacy might bring the party some attention and help reelect Representative Vito Marcantonio, a member of the American Labor Party and one of Congress's most outspoken opponents of the Cold War. He also agreed because the chance for him to speak in public had become rare.

As the anticommunist crusade intensified, DuBois stood firm. He spoke his mind at a time when few others were willing to risk it. But his career suffered as a consequence. "I found myself increasingly proscribed in pulpit, school, and platform," he noted. "My opportunity to write for publication was becoming narrower and narrower, even in the Negro press."

But as a political candidate, DuBois spoke at rallies around the New York area in front of thousands of people. The press rarely covered his speeches, but DuBois still received 200,000 votes in the election, a very respectable showing.

Although his candidacy had not received much press attention, DuBois soon found himself in the headlines. In July 1950, U.S. Secretary of State Dean Acheson claimed that the Peace Information Center was a communist-front organization and that the Stockholm Petition was a tool of the Soviet Union. DuBois shot back, "Today in this country it is becoming standard reaction to call anything 'communist' and therefore subversive and unpatriotic, which anybody for any reason dislikes." DuBois thought it ridiculous that the open exchange of ideas and freedom of speech were being limited.

The following month, the U.S. government asked the Peace Information Center to register as an agent of a foreign power. To DuBois and others at the center this was nonsense. Since they had no ties to any foreign government, they simply ignored the request. The government made repeated demands that they register, which the center kept ignoring. Eventually, the Peace Information Center disbanded, but even this did not satisfy the government.

In February 1951, DuBois and four of his colleagues were indicted for failing to register as agents of a foreign government. If convicted, each faced a possible five-year prison sentence and a

$10,000 fine. On the day of the arraignment, the slight, dignified eighty-two-year-old gentleman was led to the courtroom in handcuffs, which were removed only after his lawyer and others complained loudly. That day, DuBois said, "It is a sad commentary that we must enter a courtroom today to plead 'Not Guilty' to something that cannot be a crime—advocating peace and friendship between the American people and the peoples of the world."

The previous year, DuBois's wife, Nina, had died after a long illness. For many years, DuBois's closest friend and co-worker had been Shirley Graham, a former student. Graham, an accomplished writer and political activist, decided that they should marry because DuBois needed her support and friendship. At first DuBois scoffed, saying he was too old, but eventually he agreed. After DuBois was indicted, they moved the marriage date forward. They wanted to make sure Graham would have full privileges of meeting with him and speaking for him if he should end up in jail.

DuBois was fast approaching his eighty-third birthday. An elaborate party had been planned, to be held at the Essex House—a swanky New York hotel. After the indictment, many people who were supposed to attend suddenly changed their minds. Then the Essex House canceled their

*Shirley Graham had met DuBois when
she was a young girl in the Midwest. She became
DuBois's second wife in 1951.*

reservation. "I can stand a great deal," DuBois said later, "but this experience was rather more than I felt like bearing, especially as the blows continued to fall."

Shirley Graham went to every major hotel in Manhattan, but none were willing to rent space to honor a man the press was calling a communist.

Finally she found a restaurant in Harlem that would provide space. The 700 people who showed up may not have been as famous as those on the original guest list—many didn't even know him personally—but they were all willing to publicly express their support and admiration for DuBois. The event turned into a spirited defense of civil liberties. The famous singer and actor Paul Robeson gave a rousing speech, as did others, and birthday greetings were read from leaders across the globe.

While many of his friends had abandoned him out of fear that their own careers might be damaged, a few people stood by him. Although Vito Marcantonio had not been reelected, even with DuBois's help, he offered to defend DuBois free of charge. Many local branches of the NAACP produced resolutions supporting DuBois, but the national office was not so charitable. DuBois's old foe Walter White insisted that there was "irrefutable proof" that the center's funds had "come from Moscow" and refused to provide any support to DuBois.

In fact, the government had no such proof. Even in those hysterical times, it quickly became evident to the judge that they had no case at all. He dismissed the case before the defense had even called any witnesses.

But the damage was already done. Newspapers and magazines refused to publish DuBois's writings, and universities did not invite him to lecture. Worst of all, the United States refused to grant him visas to travel abroad. In 1953, the State Department asked him if he had ever been a communist. DuBois refused to answer. He later explained, "That is a matter of principle. I'm not a member of the Communist Party, but I think that the government has no right to ask a person to say anything about his religious views or his political views." The State Department responded by denying him a new passport.

Five years later, the U.S. Supreme Court struck down the State Department's passport restrictions. "I felt like a released prisoner," DuBois said. He quickly took advantage of his renewed freedom, and he and Shirley embarked on a world tour. Wherever they went, DuBois was showered with praise and honors. Although hardly anyone in the United States would talk to him, people everywhere else seemed to appreciate the tremendous contributions he had made. All across Europe, Russia, and China, he was greeted with rousing ovations. "This trip has completely transformed my thinking," DuBois said. "American Negroes must know what is going on in the world today, and learn for themselves what this has to

"I felt like a released prisoner."

teach them." He came back convinced that communism was the way of the future.

After a year of travel, DuBois returned to the country that preferred to forget him. But he was not comfortable. He believed that he was under surveillance and that his mail was being tampered with. After his daughter, Yolande, died in 1960, there was little to keep him in the United States.

On October 1, 1961, at age ninety-three, W. E. B. DuBois applied for membership in the Communist Party. This was a symbolic gesture—a protest against the Cold War and the anticommunist hysteria that had dominated American politics for the previous fifteen years.

Four days later, DuBois left America for good. He moved to Ghana at the invitation of President Kwame Nkrumah to work on the *Encyclopedia Africana*. "My great-grandfather was carried away in chains from the Gulf of Guinea," DuBois remarked after arriving in Africa. "I have returned that my dust shall mingle with the dust of my forefathers."

DuBois was revered in Ghana. A steady stream of visitors from around Africa and the world came to talk to the venerable old man.

"I have returned that my dust shall mingle with the dust of my forefathers."

DuBois receiving an honorary degree from the University of Ghana on his ninety-fifth birthday, February 23, 1963.

When DuBois's passport expired in 1963, the U.S. consulate in Ghana refused to renew it. He was a communist, they said. Living outside the United States and unable to get a passport, DuBois decided to renounce his U.S. citizenship. He became a citizen of Ghana.

On August 27, 1963, W. E. B. DuBois died. The following day, half a world away, 250,000 people gathered on the Mall in Washington, D.C., in a rally for civil rights. There, they heard Dr. Martin Luther King, Jr., give his famous "I have a dream" speech. They also heard Roy Wilkins, the executive director of the NAACP, announce that the grand old man of the civil rights movement had died. Wilkins, acknowledging that the relationship between his organization and DuBois had soured, said, "Regardless of the fact that in his later years, Dr. DuBois chose another path, it is incontrovertible that at the dawn of the twentieth century, his was the voice that was calling to you to gather here today in this cause."

W. E. B. DuBois's amazing life spanned nearly a century, from just after the Civil War until the 1960s. He had been a founder of the civil rights movement, the "Father of Pan-Africanism," a peace activist, and—above all—a scholar, one of the greatest of America's intellectuals. Throughout his long life, he had been at the center of remarkable changes.

Dr. Martin Luther King, Jr., on the day he delivered his "I Have a Dream" speech in Washington D.C., August 23, 1963. DuBois had died in Ghana the day before.

On February 23, 1968, what would have been DuBois's 100th birthday, Martin Luther King, Jr., gave a speech in his honor. "He saw and loved progressive humanity in all its hues—black, white, yellow, red, and brown," King said. "Dr. DuBois

has left us, but he has not died. The spirit of freedom is not buried in the grave of the valiant . . . .
Dr. DuBois's greatest virtue was his committed
empathy with all the oppressed and his divine dis-
satisfaction with all forms of injustice."

CHRONOLOGY

1868	William Edward Burghardt DuBois born in Great Barrington, Massachusetts
1884	Graduates from Great Barrington High School
1888	Graduates from Fisk University
1890	Receives B.A., cum laude, from Harvard University
1892–94	Studies at the University of Berlin
1894	Begins teaching at Wilberforce University
1895	Receives Ph.D. from Harvard University
1896	Marries Nina Gomer; begins sociological research on African-Americans in Philadelphia
1989	Becomes professor at Atlanta University
1903	Publishes *The Souls of Black Folk*
1905	Cofounds the Niagara Movement
1910	Named director of publicity and research for the National Association for the Advancement of Colored People (NAACP); founds and edits *The Crisis*

1917	Supports American involvement in World War I
1919	Organizes First Pan-African Congress
1934	Resigns from the NAACP and *The Crisis*; rejoins the faculty of Atlanta University
1935	Publishes *Black Reconstruction: An Essay toward a History of the Part which Black Folk Played in the Attempt to Reconstruct Democracy in America, 1860–1880*
1940	Founds and edits *Phylon*
1944	Rejoins the NAACP as director of special research
1945	Becomes a consultant to the U.S. delegation at the founding of the United Nations
1948	Resigns from the NAACP
1950	Nina DuBois dies; W. E. B. DuBois runs for U.S. Senate on the American Labor Party ticket
1951	Marries Shirley Graham; as an officer of the Peace Information Center, Du Bois is tried and acquitted of failing to register as a foreign agent
1952	Denied U.S. passport
1958	Begins world tour, including U.S.S.R. and China
1961	Joins American Communist Party; moves to Ghana to begin work on the *Encyclopedia Africana*
1963	Becomes citizen of Ghana; dies in Accra, Ghana, on August 27

A NOTE ON SOURCES

The most detailed biography of W. E. B. DuBois is David Levering Lewis's Pulitzer Prize-winning *W. E. B.: Biography of a Race, 1868–1919* (New York: Henry Holt, 1993). Although the book covers only the first half of DuBois's monumental life, Lewis uncovered many new details about DuBois and provides fresh insight into his personal and intellectual development.

Manning Marable's *W. E. B. DuBois: Black Radical Democrat* (Boston: Twayne, 1986) is good shorter adult biography, which focuses on DuBois's political ideas. Also useful are Virginia Hamilton's *W. E. B. DuBois: A Biography* (New York: HarperCollins, 1972) and Mark Stafford's *W. E. B. DuBois: Scholar and Activist* (New York: Chelsea House, 1989), two young adult biographies that give thorough, interesting accounts of his life.

DuBois's own writing sometimes provides a more personal view of the man. *The Souls of Black Folk* (New York: Vintage, 1990) is a classic, which shows off his grace, spirit, and towering intelligence.

FOR MORE INFORMATION

BOOKS

DuBois, W. E. B. *The Souls of Black Folk*. New York: Vintage, 1990.

———. *W. E. B. DuBois Speaks: Speeches and Addresses, 1890–1919*. Edited by Philip S. Foner. New York: Pathfinder, 1970,

Hamilton, Virginia. *W. E. B. DuBois: A Biography*. New York: HarperCollins, 1972.

Lawler, Mary. *Marcus Garvey: Black Nationalist Leader*. New York: Chelsea House, 1988.

Marable, Manning. *W. E. B. DuBois: Black Radical Democrat*. Boston: Twayne, 1986.

Schroeder, Alan. *Booker T. Washington: Educator and Racial Spokesman*. New York: Chelsea House, 1992.

Stafford, Mark. *W. E. B. DuBois: Scholar and Activist*. New York: Chelsea House, 1989.

INTERNET

The W. E. B. DuBois Virtual University
http://www.members.tripod.com/~dubois
This website contains biographical information, an extensive bibliography, and some writings by and about DuBois.

The W.E.B. DuBois Society
http://wwwerols.com/tdpedu/dubois/dubois.htm
Sponsored by Albert Einstein High School, Silver Spring, Maryland, this page has biographical details, a calendar of events, and a profile of the society and school.

W.E.B. DuBois Institute for Afro-American Research
http://web-dubois.fas.harvard.edu/
Named for its famous alumnus, this site gives information on lectures, research projects, working groups, and fellowships.

"Voices Which Shaped Our Times"
http://www.msu.edu/course/mc/112/1920s/Garvey-Dubois/index.html
Profiles of two pioneering African American leaders of the early twentieth century, with bio's, papers, images, and links.

INDEX

Numbers in *italics* indicate illustrations.

ABOUT THE AUTHOR

Melissa McDaniel is the author of many books for young people, including *Spike Lee: On His Own Terms*, for Franklin Watts. She lives in New York City.